KB034002

가장
알기 쉽게
배우는

초등

기본영어

폭넓은
영어 회화
실생활
기본문장 수록

STEP BY STEP BOOK 2(문형)

가장 알기 쉽게 배우는

초등 기본 영어

STEP BY STEP BOOK 2(문형)

저 자 방정인
발행인 고본화
발 행 반석출판사
2020년 6월 15일 초판 1쇄 인쇄
2020년 6월 20일 초판 1쇄 발행
홈페이지 www.bansok.co.kr
이메일 bansok@bansok.co.kr
블로그 blog.naver.com/bansokbooks

07547 서울시 강서구 양천로 583. B동 1007호
(서울시 강서구 염창동 240-21번지 우림블루나인 비즈니스센터 B동 1007호)
대표전화 02) 2093-3399 **팩 스** 02) 2093-3393
출 판 부 02) 2093-3395 **영업부** 02) 2093-3396
등록번호 제315-2008-000033호

ISBN 978-89-7172-918-2 (63740)

반석출판사
Bansok

머리말

국제 개방 시대를 맞아 생활 영어회화의 필요성은 날로 증대하고 있습니다.

초·중학교 영어 교육 방향이 문법과 독해 위주에서 회화 위주의 교육으로 방향 전환됩니다. 더욱이 1996년부터 초등학교에 영어가 정규 과목으로 채택되면서 초등학교 영어는 회화 위주로 교육되고 있습니다.

문법은 영어를 효율적으로 배우는 데 필요한 과정의 한 부분입니다. 영어 교육은 읽고 내용을 파악할 능력을 갖춘 후, 영어를 듣고 자기의 의사를 상대방에게 정확히 전달할 수 있는 능력을 갖추게 해야 합니다.

그런데 그동안의 영어 교육은 영어를 듣고 말할 수 있는 능력을 교육하지 못했습니다. 그래서 앞으로 영어회화를 효율적이고 성공적으로 교육하기 위해서는 교육 프로그램과 교사의 영어회화 능력을 증진시켜야겠습니다. 가장 중요한 것은 우리나라 학생들에게 알맞은 영어회화 교재와 교육 방법의 출현입니다. 그동안 거의 모든 영어회화 교재는 성인을 위한 내용으로 일관되어 있었습니다.

반석출판사에서는 초등학생을 위한 생활 영어회화 교재인 『초등 기본 영어 STEP BY STEP』을 저술하게 되었습니다.

『초등 기본 영어 STEP BY STEP BOOK 1』(입문)은 영어회화 기초로서 구어체 중심으로 실생활 영어를 수록하였습니다. 초등학생을 위한 기초 영어회화 교재로 구성하였습니다.

『초등 기본 영어 STEP BY STEP BOOK 2』(문형)은 『초등 기본 영어 STEP BY STEP BOOK 1』(입문)을 기초로 대화의 폭을 넓혔습니다. 『초등 기본 영어 STEP BY STEP BOOK 1』(입문)을 마치거나 수준 높은 학생을 위하여 초등학생들의 생활상을 다루었습니다.

영어 듣기와 영어 말하기의 성공을 위해서는 Native Speaker와 회화 공부를 하는 것도 좋지만 현실적으로 가장 이상적인 방법은 음원을 활용한 회화교육입니다. 회화교육도 반복 교육만이 유일한 길입니다.

끝으로 『초등 기본 영어 STEP BY STEP』을 통해 영어회화 교육에 성공하기를 기원하는 바입니다.

저자 **방 정 인**

목차

LESSON

CLASSROOM ENGLISH

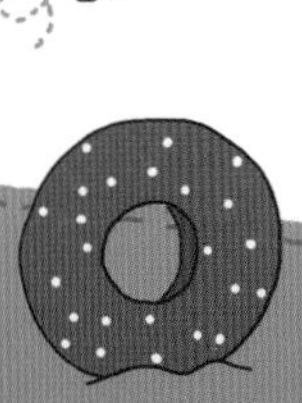

이 책의 특징

『초등 기본 영어 STEP BY STEP BOOK 2』에 오신 것을 환영합니다. 이 책은 『초등 기본 영어 STEP BY STEP BOOK 1』에 이어 조금 더 긴 대화를 공부할 수 있는 책이랍니다.

이 책은 초등학생의 생활에서 만날 수 있는 여러 가지 상황들을 다루고 있어요. 아침에 일어나는 것부터 씻고 아침밥 먹기, 집을 나서면서, 길에서 친구들을 만났을 때 등등 다양한 상황들에서 할 수 있는 영어회화, 혹은 영어로 된 대화들을 다루고 있는 것이지요.

이 책에서는 그림에 직접 영어로 된 대화문이 들어 있어요. 마치 만화처럼 말이에요. 그래서 일반적인 대화만이 아니라 특정 인물이 실제로 말하는 대화를 접할 수 있답니다. 책과 함께 제공되는 mp3 음원을 통해 어린이는 대화를 먼저 들어보고, 또 따라서 읽어볼 수 있어요. 책의 아래 칸에는 대화 중에서 궁금할 수 있는 사항들이 정리되어 있어서 이해를 도울 거예요.

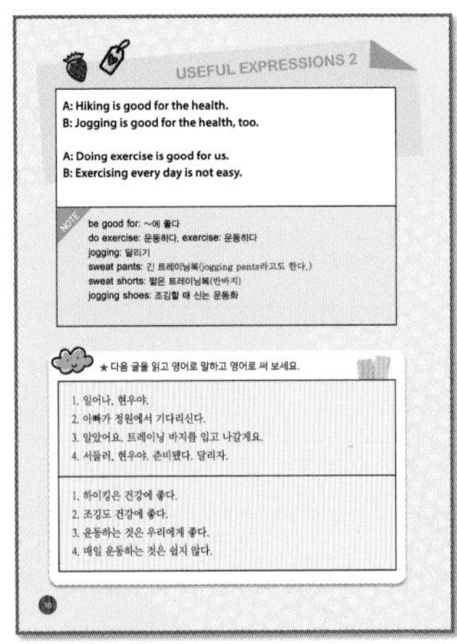

USEFUL EXPRESSIONS 2

A: Hiking is good for the health.
B: Jogging is good for the health, too.

A: Doing exercise is good for us.
B: Exercising every day is not easy.

NOTE
be good for: ~에 좋다
do exercise: 운동하다, exercise: 운동하다
jogging: 달리기
sweat pants: 긴 트레이닝복(jogging pants라고도 한다.)
sweat shorts: 짧은 트레이닝복(반바지)
jogging shoes: 조깅할 때 신는 운동화

★ 다음 글을 읽고 영어로 말하고 영어로 써 보세요.

1. 일어나, 현우야.
2. 아빠가 정원에서 기다리신다.
3. 알았어요. 트레이닝 바지를 입고 나갈게요.
4. 서둘러, 현우야. 준비됐다. 달리자.

1. 하이킹은 건강에 좋다.
2. 조깅도 건강에 좋다.
3. 운동하는 것은 우리에게 좋다.
4. 매일 운동하는 것은 쉽지 않다.

첫 번째 대화가 끝난 후, 어린이는 유용한 표현들이라는 이름으로 두 번째 대화를 공부할 수 있어요. 앞서와 비슷한 상황에서 말할 수 있는 또 다른 내용이 등장하죠. 역시 이 대화도 먼저 듣고 따라 읽어볼 수 있게 되어 있어요. 대화의 아래에는 역시 궁금할 수 있는 사항들이 설명되어 있답니다.

마지막으로는 한글로 제시되어 있는 대화문을 영어로 말하고 영어로 써 보는 연습을 하게 되어 있어요. 이를 통해 어린이는 앞서 공부한 내용들을 다시 한 번 기억해 볼 수 있는 시간을 갖게 돼요.

교실 영어 1

S 선생님, 안녕하세요.
T 여러분, 안녕하세요. 오늘 아침은 어때요?
S 좋아요, 고맙습니다. 선생님은 어떠세요?
T 좋아요, 고마워요. 조용히 해라, 지훈아.
S 죄송합니다.
T 너희들 숙제해 왔니?
S 예, 했어요.
T 숙제를 내 보렴.
S 여기 있어요.
T 너희들은 착한 학생이로구나.

CLASSROOM ENGLISH 1

S Good morning, sir.
T Good morning, class. How are you this morning?
S We are just fine. Thank you. And you?
T Fine, thanks. Stop talking, Ji-hoon.
S I'm sorry.
T Did you do your homework?
S Yes, we did.
T Hand in your homework.
S Here it is.
T You are good students.

이렇게 구성된 하나의 과는 총 44개의 상황들로 확장된답니다. 우리는 이를 통해 다양한 상황별 대화들을 공부할 수 있게 돼요. 그리고 44개의 대화를 모두 공부한 후에는 학교 교실에서 선생님과 할 수 있는 대화 7개를 만나게 돼요. 이렇게 해서 어린이는 일상생활과 학교생활 중에 말해 볼 수 있는 영어 대화들을 익히게 된답니다.

어때요? 부모님과 형제들, 친구들과 선생님과 함께 영어회화를 말해보고 싶지 않나요? 우리 모두 얼른 공부를 시작해 보아요.

IN THE BEDROOM 1

Wake up, Ji-min.

Okay, Mom.

Good morning, Ji-min.

Good morning, Mom.

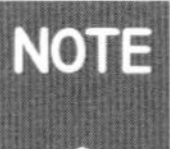

wake up: 깨우다

Okay. = O.K.: 알았습니다.

Good morning.: 안녕하세요.(아침인사)

USEFUL EXPRESSIONS 1

A: Wake up, wake up, Min-jae.
B: I'm sleepy, Mom.

A: We're going on a picnic to the Seoul Grand Park today.
B: I'm up already.

NOTE

I'm sleepy.: 잠이 온다(잠이 덜 깬 상태)
go on a picnic: 소풍 가다
the Seoul Grand Park: 서울대공원
Great! / Wow! 등은 좋아서 놀라는 표현이다.
I'm up already. 벌써 일어났어.(아이들이 흔히 쓰는 말)
I've already gotten up. 벌써 일어났어.
(어른들 사이에서 정중한 표현으로 쓰인다.)

★ 다음 글을 읽고 영어로 말하고 영어로 써 보세요.

1. 일어나, 지민아.
2. 알았어요, 엄마.
3. 잘 잤니, 지민아.
4. 안녕히 주무셨어요, 엄마.

1. 일어나, 일어나, 민재야.
2. 엄마, 졸려.
3. 우린 오늘 서울대공원으로 소풍 갈 거야.
4. 저 벌써 일어났어요.

IN THE BEDROOM 2

Wake up, Hyun-woo. Dad is waiting for you in the garden.

O.K. I'll wear my sweat pants and go out.

Hurry up, Hyun-woo. I'm ready. Let's run.

NOTE

wait for: ~를 기다리다

sweat pants: 트레이닝 바지(운동복)

I'm ready.: 준비됐다.

USEFUL EXPRESSIONS 2

A: Hiking is good for the health.
B: Jogging is good for the health, too.

A: Doing exercise is good for us.
B: Exercising every day is not easy.

NOTE

be good for: ~에 좋다
do exercise: 운동하다, exercise: 운동하다
jogging: 달리기
sweat pants: 긴 트레이닝복(jogging pants라고도 한다.)
sweat shorts: 짧은 트레이닝복(반바지)
jogging shoes: 조깅할 때 신는 운동화

★ 다음 글을 읽고 영어로 말하고 영어로 써 보세요.

1. 일어나, 현우야.
2. 아빠가 정원에서 기다리신다.
3. 알았어요. 트레이닝 바지를 입고 나갈게요.
4. 서둘러, 현우야. 준비됐다. 달리자.

1. 하이킹은 건강에 좋다.
2. 조깅도 건강에 좋다.
3. 운동하는 것은 우리에게 좋다.
4. 매일 운동하는 것은 쉽지 않다.

LESSON 3(THREE)

IN THE BATHROOM 1

Wash your face and brush your teeth.

All right.

Your towel.

Thanks, Mom.

NOTE all right = alright: 좋습니다. 상대방의 말을 승낙할 때 쓴다.
All right. / O.K. / Why not? 등도 같은 뜻으로 쓰인다.
Your towel. = Here is your towel.: 여기에 너의 세수수건이 있다.

USEFUL EXPRESSIONS 3

A: Did you wash your hair?
B: No, I didn't.

A: Don't forget to wash your hair every day.
B: Yes, Mom.

NOTE

Don't forget.: 잊지 말라. ………………………(부정명령문)

명령문의 예)	Go home.	집에 가라.
	Don't go home.	집에 가지 마라.
	Let's go home.	집에 가자.
	Let's not go home.	집에 가지 말자.

★ 다음 글을 읽고 영어로 말하고 영어로 써 보세요.

1. 세수하고 이를 닦으렴.
2. 알았어요.
3. 네 세수수건이야.
4. 고맙습니다, 엄마.

---

1. 머리 감았니?
2. 아니, 안 감았어요.
3. 매일 머리 감는 것을 잊어버리지 마라.
4. 예, 엄마.

IN THE BATHROOM 2

NOTE

take a shower: 샤워를 하다

piss: 오줌 누다, 소변

Wait a minute.: 잠깐만 기다리세요.

USEFUL EXPRESSIONS 4

A: Come out quickly.
B: All right. I'm trying.

A: You're always in the bathroom for a long time.
B: How about you?

NOTE

'소변 보다'의 여러 가지 표현들
piss: 오줌 누다(10세 미만 아이들 사이에 흔히 쓰인다.)
pee: 오줌 누다(10대 사이에 흔히 쓰이는 말이다.)
have a leak: 소변을 보다(가까운 사이에 쓰이는 말이다.)
use the bathroom[toilet/washroom]: 화장실을 사용하다
urinate: 소변을 보다(의학적인 표현이다.)
How about you?는 너도 화장실에 오래 있지 않았냐는 항의의 표현이다.

★ 다음 글을 읽고 영어로 말하고 영어로 써 보세요.

1. 너 뭘 하고 있니?
2. 나 샤워하고 있어.
3. 뭐라고? 난 지금 당장 소변을 봐야 해.
4. 잠깐만 기다려.

1. 빨리 나와.
2. 알았어. 노력 중이야.
3. 넌 화장실에 항상 오래 있더라.
4. 넌 안 그러니?

LESSON 5(FIVE)

THE BREAKFAST TABLE 1

The breakfast is ready.

Is that my toast?

Yes, it is. It's for you.

Pass that to me.

NOTE

The breakfast is ready.: 아침 식사 준비됐다.

It's for you.: 네가 먹을 것이다.

Pass that to me.: 저것을 제게 건네주세요.

Would you pass that to me? 저것을 저에게 건네주시겠어요?

USEFUL EXPRESSIONS 5

A: Do you like this hamburger?
B: Yes, I do. It tastes good.

A: More please.
B: No. You'll get a stomachache.

NOTE

It tastes good. = It is delicious.: 맛이 좋다
More please. = Give me more please.: 많이 주세요.
* 통증의 여러 가지 표현들: stomachache: 복통
toothache: 치통
headache: 두통
backache: 등의 아픔, 요통

★ 다음 글을 읽고 영어로 말하고 영어로 써 보세요.

1. 아침 식사 준비됐다.
2. 저것이 제 토스트예요?
3. 그래, 네가 먹을 것이다.
4. 저것을 저에게 건네주세요.

1. 너는 이 햄버거를 좋아하니?
2. 응, 그래. 맛이 좋아.
3. 좀 더 줄래.
4. 안 돼. 배가 아플 거야.

THE BREAKFAST TABLE 2

This bean paste soup is delicious.

Thank you.

Give me some more, please.

All right, but only a little more.

NOTE

bean paste soup: 된장국

bean sprouts: 콩나물

only a little more: 조금만 더

USEFUL EXPRESSIONS 6

A: This pizza tastes very good.
B: Do you want another slice?

A: No, thank you. I'm full.
B: You're right. It's not good to eat too much.

NOTE

another slice: 또 한 쪽
another: 다른, 또 하나의　　slice: 조각(piece)
No, thank you.: 아니, 괜찮습니다.(사양할 때 쓰이는 말이다.)
I'm full.: 배가 부르다.(배가 부른 상태)
I had enough.: 배가 부르다.(충분히 먹었다는 뜻이다.)
It's not good to eat too much.에서 It은 가주어이고, to eat은 진주어이다. 이것을 〈it ~ to부정사〉의 구문이라고 한다.

★ 다음 글을 읽고 영어로 말하고 영어로 써 보세요.

1. 이 된장국은 맛이 있어요.
2. 고맙다.
3. 좀 더 주세요.
4. 그래, 하지만 조금만이야.

1. 이 피자 무척 맛이 있네요.
2. 한 조각 더 먹을래?
3. 아니, 괜찮아요. 배불러요.
4. 네 말이 맞다. 많이 먹는 것은 좋지 않아.

THE BREAKFAST TABLE 3

May I have some more rice?

All right. Hand me your bowl.

Thank you, Mom.

Don't eat too fast. Take your time.

NOTE

rice: 밥, 쌀

Hand me your bowl.: 밥그릇을 달라.(밥그릇을 손으로 건네 달라는 표현이다.)

Take your time: 천천히 먹어.(서둘지 말고 천천히 먹으라는 뜻이다.)

USEFUL EXPRESSIONS 7

A: Would you like some meat?
B: Give me a little.

A: Do you want some bread?
B: Yes. Put some jam on it, please.

NOTE

Would you like some meat?	고기 좀 드시겠어요?(정중한 표현)
Do you want some meat?	고기 좀 먹겠니?

Put some jam on it.에서 it은 위의 bread이다.

May I have some more rice?	밥 좀 더 먹어도 돼요?(상대방의 허락을 묻는 말이다.)

먹다: eat, have, take 등

★ 다음 글을 읽고 영어로 말하고 영어로 써 보세요.

1. 밥 좀 더 주실래요?
2. 그래, 밥그릇을 건네주렴.
3. 감사합니다, 엄마.
4. 너무 빨리 먹지 마라. 천천히 먹어.

1. 고기 좀 드시겠어요?
2. 조금만 주세요.
3. 빵 좀 드시겠어요?
4. 예, 빵 위에 잼 좀 발라주세요.

LESSON 8(EIGHT)

THE BREAKFAST TABLE 4

NOTE a cup of coffee: 커피 한 잔　　a glass of milk: 우유 한 잔

Here it is.: 여기에 있다.

Here you are.: 여기에 있습니다.

둘 다 같은 뜻으로 쓰인다.

USEFUL EXPRESSIONS 8

A: Ice cream or fruit for dessert?
B: Fruit, please.

A: What kind of fruit do you like?
B: I like grapes.

NOTE

a cup of tea: 차 한 잔
a glass of orange juice: 오렌지주스 한 잔
a piece of bread: 빵 한 조각
a slice of pizza: 피자 한 조각
for dessert: 후식으로
for lunch: 점심으로
for breakfast: 아침 식사로

★ 다음 글을 읽고 영어로 말하고 영어로 써 보세요.

1. 커피 좀 드시겠습니까?
2. 물론이지요, 커피 한 잔 주세요.
3. 여기 있습니다.
4. 고맙습니다.

1. 아이스크림이나 과일 중에 디저트로 뭘 하시겠어요?
2. 과일이요.
3. 어떤 과일을 좋아하세요?
4. 나는 포도를 좋아해요.

BEFORE LEAVING HOME 1

NOTE

It is raining now.: 지금 비가 오고 있다.
(현재 비가 계속 오고 있는 상태)

It rains today.: 오늘 비가 온다.(비가 오는 동작)

It is rainy today.: 오늘 비가 온다.(비가 오는 상태)

USEFUL EXPRESSIONS 9

A: It is cold today.
B: I'll wear the sweater.

A: Watch out on the ice.
B: Don't worry.

NOTE

It is cold. 춥다
It is warm. 따뜻하다
It is hot. 덥다
It is chilly. 싸늘하다
Look out. = Watch out.: 위험해, 조심해.
on the ice: 빙판 위에서

★ 다음 글을 읽고 영어로 말하고 영어로 써 보세요.

1. 지금 비가 오고 있다.
2. 제 우산 어디에 있어요?
3. 현관에 있는 바구니에 있다.
4. 알았어요, 찾았어요.

1. 오늘은 춥다.
2. 스웨터를 입을게요.
3. 빙판에서 조심해.
4. 걱정 마세요.

BEFORE LEAVING HOME 2

Hurry up, Ji-min.

What time is it now?

It's eight.

I must hurry to school.

NOTE

What time is it now?

It is eight o'clock.

It은 시간을 나타내는 비인칭주어로 해석하지 않는다.

USEFUL EXPRESSIONS 10

A: When are you coming home?
B: About four.

A: Watch out for cars.
B: All right, don't worry about me.

NOTE

When are you coming home? 언제 집에 올 거니?
〈be + 현재분사〉: 진행의 뜻이 있지만 여기서는 미래의 뜻이 있다.
e.g) He is coming home soon. 그는 집에 곧 올 것이다.
He is leaving home soon. 그는 곧 집을 떠날 것이다.
He is going to school soon. 그는 곧 학교에 갈 것이다.
He is arriving at home. 그는 집에 도착할 것이다.
Watch out for cars. = Look out for cars.: 차들을 조심해라.

★ 다음 글을 읽고 영어로 말하고 영어로 써 보세요.

1. 지민아, 서둘러라.
2. 지금 몇 시예요?
3. 8시야.
4. 서둘러서 학교에 가야겠다.

1. 언제 집에 올 거니?
2. 약 4시에요.
3. 차를 조심해라.
4. 알았어요. 제 걱정 마세요.

LESSON 11(ELEVEN)

IN THE STREET 1

Hi.

Hello. How are you?

Fine, thank you. And you?

I'm fine, thank you.

NOTE Hi와 Hello는 오전 오후 구별 없이 자주 쓰이는 인사말이다.
How are you? 어떻게 지내세요?(안부를 묻는 말이다.)
And you? = And how are you?의 준말이다.

USEFUL EXPRESSIONS 11

A: How are you this morning?
B: I'm fine, thanks. And how are you?

A: I'm fine, too.
B: Let's go to school quickly.

NOTE

만났을 때의 여러 가지 인사들
Good morning. 안녕하세요.(오전 인사)
Good afternoon. 안녕하세요.(오후 인사)
Good evening. 안녕하세요.(저녁 인사)
Hi. 안녕.(오전 오후 구별 없이 사용)
Hello. 안녕.(오전 오후 구별 없이 사용)
How are you? 어떻게 지내세요?(건강이나 기분을 묻는 인사)

★ 다음 글을 읽고 영어로 말하고 영어로 써 보세요.

1. 안녕.
2. 안녕. 어떻게 지냈니?
3. 잘 있어, 고마워. 너는 어때?
4. 난 잘 있어, 고마워.

---

1. 오늘 아침은 어때?
2. 좋아, 고마워. 너는 어때?
3. 나도 좋아.
4. 학교에 빨리 가자.

LESSON 12(TWELVE)

IN THE STREET 2

Hello, Mi-ae.

Hi, Ji-min.

We're late for school this morning.

That's right. Let's run to school.

NOTE

A: Hi.	A: Hello.	A: Hi.	A: Hello.
B: Hi.	B: Hello.	B: Hello.	B: Hi.

Hi와 Hello는 오전 오후 구별 없이 자주 쓰이는 가벼운 인사이다.

USEFUL EXPRESSIONS 12

A: We're late today.
B: How about taking a bus?

A: That's a good idea.
B: A bus is coming here.

NOTE

be late: 늦다
be late for: ~에 늦다
take a bus: 버스를 타다
get on the bus: 버스를 타다
get off the bus: 버스에서 내리다
That's a good idea.: 그거 좋은 생각이다.
A bus is coming.은 미래의 뜻이 아니고 진행의 뜻이다.

★ 다음 글을 읽고 영어로 말하고 영어로 써 보세요.

1. 안녕, 미애.
2. 안녕, 지민.
3. 오늘 아침은 학교에 늦었다.
3. 맞아. 학교로 빨리 달려가자.

1. 오늘 늦었어.
2. 버스를 타는 것이 어때?
3. 그거 좋은 생각이다.
4. 버스가 이곳으로 오고 있어.

LESSON 13(THIRTEEN)

IN THE CLASSROOM 1

Good morning, class.

Good morning, sir.

Let's start our class.

Yes, sir. It's Lesson 5.

NOTE 선생님이 학생들을 부를 때: class / everyone / everybody 등이 있다.

학생들이 선생님을 부를 때: sir / ma'am / Mr. Kim / Ms. Kim 등이 있다.

USEFUL EXPRESSIONS 13

A: Open your books to page 15.
B: Yes, ma'am.

A: Did you do your homework?
B: Yes, we did.

NOTE

Open your books to page 15.에서 전치사 to를 주의하라.
do one's homework: 숙제를 하다
* 평서문과 의문문

You do your homework.	You did your homework.
Do you do your homework?	Did you do your homework?

Did you do your homework?에서 you는 너희들(복수)의 뜻이다.

★ 다음 글을 읽고 영어로 말하고 영어로 써 보세요.

1. 여러분, 안녕하세요?
2. 선생님, 안녕하세요?
3. 수업을 시작합시다.
4. 예, 선생님. 제5과입니다.

1. 여러분의 책 15페이지를 펴세요.
2. 예, 선생님.
3. 너희들 숙제했니?
4. 예, 했습니다.

IN THE CLASSROOM 2

NOTE

Stop talking. 조용히 해.

Look at me.: 나를 봐.

at the beginning of Lesson 5: 5과 처음부터

USEFUL EXPRESSIONS 14

A: Be quiet, everyone. Hyun-woo, speak up.
B: Yes, ma'am.

A: Good. You're a good reader.
B: Thank you, ma'am.

NOTE

조용히 하라는 표현들

Stop talking. Be quiet.

Quiet down. Don't make a noise.

큰 소리로 말하라는 여러 가지 표현들

Speak up. Speak loudly.

You are a good reader. = You can read very well.

잘 읽는다는 표현들이다.

★ 다음 글을 읽고 영어로 말하고 영어로 써 보세요.

1. 조용히 해라. 현우야, 날 보렴.
2. 죄송합니다, 선생님.
3. 5과 처음부터 읽어보아라.
4. 제5과, 아침 식사가 준비되었습니다.

1. 여러분, 조용히 하세요. 현우야, 크게 읽어보렴.
2. 예, 선생님.
3. 좋아요, 잘 읽었어요.
4. 감사합니다, 선생님.

LESSON 15(FIFTEEN)

LUNCHTIME 1

It's time to have lunch.

Let me see your food tray.

Wow! Your lunch looks very delicious.

Thanks. Today is my birthday.

NOTE

It's time to have lunch. 점심 먹을 시간이다.

to have 부정사는 time을 꾸미는 형용사적 용법으로 쓰였다.

Let me see your food tray. 네 점심 식판 좀 보자.

USEFUL EXPRESSIONS 15

A: Let's have lunch with me.
B: O.K. I'll bring some water.

A: Thank you. I want cold water.
B: Here it is.

NOTE

시제의 여러 가지 예

I bring some water. .... (현재)
I brought some water. .... (과거)
I will bring some water. .... (미래)
I am bringing some water. .... (현재진행)
I was bringing some water. .... (과거진행)
I have brought some water. .... (현재완료)

★ 다음 글을 읽고 영어로 말하고 영어로 써 보세요.

1. 점심 먹을 시간이다.
2. 네 점심 식판 좀 보자.
3. 와! 네 점심 맛있어 보이는구나.
4. 고마워. 오늘이 내 생일이야.

1. 나와 같이 점심을 먹자.
2. 좋아. 내가 물 좀 가져올게.
3. 고마워, 난 찬물을 마실래.
4. 여기 있어.

LUNCHTIME 2

NOTE 식당을 표현하는 말들

dining room: 식당(가정, 호텔 등의 전용 식당)

restaurant: 음식점

cafeteria: 학교 식당(self service 식당)

USEFUL EXPRESSIONS 16

A: Which food do you like better?
B: I like pizza better than hamburger.

A: Pizza is more expensive than hamburger.
B: Don't worry. I have some money to buy pizza.

NOTE

비교급과 최상급의 변화

원급	비교급	최상급
old	older	oldest
big	bigger	biggest
good(well)	better	best
many(much)	more	most
expensive	more expensive	most expensive
beautiful	more beautiful	most beautiful

★ 다음 글을 읽고 영어로 말하고 영어로 써 보세요.

1. 오늘 점심으로 뭐니?
2. 글쎄, 모르겠는데. 식당으로 서둘러 가자.
3. 샌드위치와 사과야.
4. 빨리 먹고 나가자.

1. 너는 어떤 음식을 더 좋아하니?
2. 난 햄버거보다 피자가 더 좋아.
3. 피자는 햄버거보다 더 비싸.
4. 걱정 마. 피자 사 먹을 돈이 좀 있어.

THE SCHOOL YARD 1

NOTE

hide-and-seek: 술래잡기
tagger: 술래
Ready go.: 준비 시작

USEFUL EXPRESSIONS 17

A: How about leapfrog?
B: Okay, good.

A: You are too heavy.
B: Don't worry. I'm on a diet.

NOTE

여러 가지 놀이 종류
hide–and–seek: 술래잡기
leapfrog: 등 짚고 넘기(말타기)
skipping: 줄넘기
dodgeball: 볼로 맞히기(피구)
see–saw: 시소
swing: 그네

★ 다음 글을 읽고 영어로 말하고 영어로 써 보세요.

1. 술래잡기하자.
2. 좋은 생각이야. 내가 친구들을 모을게.
3. 내가 술래가 될게.
4. 좋아. 준비 시작.

1. 말타기 어때?
2. 그래, 좋지.
3. 넌 너무 무거워.
4. 걱정하지 마. 다이어트 중이야.

LESSON 18(EIGHTEEN)

THE SCHOOL YARD 2

Did you bring a skipping rope?

Yes, I brought it. Let's skip.

Can you skip well?

Yes, I can. Of course. I can skip better than any other girls.

NOTE skipping (game): 줄넘기
skipping rope: 줄넘기 줄

USEFUL EXPRESSIONS 18

A: How about a game with a ball?
B: All right.

A: Let's play dodgeball.
B: The bell is ringing. Let's go into the classroom quickly.

NOTE

dodgeball: 피구
with a ball: 공을 가지고
go into = enter: 들어가다
play baseball: 야구를 하다
play basketball: 농구를 하다
play volleyball: 배구를 하다
play soccer: 축구를 하다

★ 다음 글을 읽고 영어로 말하고 영어로 써 보세요.

1. 너 줄넘기 가져왔니?
2. 응, 가져왔어. 줄넘기하자.
3. 너 줄넘기 잘할 수 있니?
4. 응, 그래. 물론이지. 난 다른 어떤 소녀보다도 줄넘기를 잘할 수 있어.

1. 공 가지고 게임하는 거 어때요?
2. 좋아.
3. 피구하자.
4. 종이 울리고 있다. 빨리 교실로 들어가자.

LESSON 19(NINETEEN)

BACK IN THE CLASSROOM

I don't like math. It's difficult for me.

Me, neither. I like social studies better.

Stop talking, Ji-min and Mi-ae.

I'm sorry. I'll be quiet.

NOTE I don't like math.

Me, neither. 나 역시 수학을 좋아하지 않는다.

= I don't like math, either.

USEFUL EXPRESSIONS 19

A: I like science. I want to be a scientist.
B: Me, too.

A: My dad bought me a computer on my birthday.
B: Let's go to my home and play computer games.

NOTE

4형식에서 간접목적어와 직접목적어를 바꿀 때
My dad bought me a computer.
My dad bought a computer for me.
My dad gave me a camera.
My dad gave a camera to me.
My dad asked me a question.
My dad asked a question of me.

★ 다음 글을 읽고 영어로 말하고 영어로 써 보세요.

1. 나는 수학을 좋아하지 않아. 수학은 나에게 어려워.
2. 나도 그래. 나는 사회를 더 좋아해.
3. 조용히 해. 지민아, 미애야.
4. 죄송합니다. 조용히 하겠습니다.

1. 나는 과학을 좋아한다. 나는 과학자가 되고 싶어.
2. 나도 그래.
3. 아빠가 내 생일에 컴퓨터를 사 주셨어.
4. 우리 집에 가서 컴퓨터 게임을 하자.

FREE TIME AFTER SCHOOL 1

NOTE

play basketball: 농구를 하다
play football: 축구를 하다
play table tennis: 탁구를 하다

USEFUL EXPRESSIONS 20

A: How about going to a basketball game?
B: That's a good idea.

A: I like Huh-hoon, the best basketball player.
B: That's right. He is this season's basketball MVP.

NOTE

인칭대명사의 격변화

주격	소유격	목적격	소유대명사
I	my	me	mine
you	your	you	yours
he	his	him	his
she	her	her	hers
we	our	us	ours
they	their	them	theirs

★ 다음 글을 읽고 영어로 말하고 영어로 써 보세요.

1. 농구를 하자.
2. 미안해. 난 숙제를 해야 해.
3. 나중에 숙제를 하자.
4. 좋아. 한 시간만 놀자.

1. 농구 경기에 가 보는 것 어때?
2. 그거 좋은 생각이다.
3, 난 최고의 농구 선수 허훈을 좋아해.
4. 맞아. 그는 금년도 농구 MVP이다.

LESSON 21(TWENTY-ONE)

FREE TIME AFTER SCHOOL 2

Let's go and get some ice cream.

What kind of ice cream do you like?

I like strawberry ice cream.

I want to have vanilla and chocolate ice cream.

NOTE Let's go and get some ice cream.에서 go and get = go to get: 먹으러 가다

vanilla and chocolate ice cream: 바닐라와 초콜릿이 섞인 아이스크림

USEFUL EXPRESSIONS 21

A: I'm hungry. How about tteokbokki?
B: That's good. Tteokbokki is my favorite food.

A: Don't eat too fast. There are only a few on the plate.
B: O.K, but you, too.

NOTE

tteokbokki: 떡볶이
favorite: 좋아하는
a few: 약간의, 몇몇의
few: 거의 ~ 않다
but you, too. = but you don't eat too fast, too.
only a few: 단지 몇 개만
plate: 가운데가 푹 들어가지 않은 접시
dish: 가운데가 푹 들어간 접시

★ 다음 글을 읽고 영어로 말하고 영어로 써 보세요.

1. 아이스크림 먹으러 가자.
2. 너는 어떤 아이스크림을 좋아하니?
3. 나는 딸기 아이스크림이 좋아.
4. 나는 바닐라 초콜릿 아이스크림을 먹고 싶어.

1. 난 배고파. 떡볶이 어떠니?
2. 좋아. 떡볶이는 내가 좋아하는 음식이야.
3. 너무 빨리 먹지 마. 접시에 몇 개밖에 없잖아.
4. 알았어, 하지만 너도 빨리 먹지 마.

BACK HOME 1

NOTE

I'm home.: 다녀왔습니다.

Come on in: 들어와라(문이 열렸을 때)

Come in: 들어와라(문이 닫혔을 때)

Here is some pizza you like.에서 you like는 pizza를 꾸미는 형용사절

USEFUL EXPRESSIONS 22

A: How's your English Speech Contest?
B: I got a first prize at the English Speech Contest.

A: Congratulations!
B: Thank you very much. I'm lucky.

NOTE

English Speech Contest: 영어 웅변대회
got a first prize: 1등상을 탔다
Congratulations!: 축하합니다!
Congratulations on you.: 당신에게 축하를 드립니다.
I'm lucky: 나는 운이 좋다
I'm happy: 나는 행복하다
lucky는 운이 따랐을 때 쓰인다.

★ 다음 글을 읽고 영어로 말하고 영어로 써 보세요.

1. 엄마, 다녀왔습니다.
2. 들어와라. 배고프지?
3. 네, 엄마. 무척 배고파요.
4. 여기 네가 좋아하는 피자가 있다.

1. 영어 웅변대회가 어땠어요?
2. 나는 영어 웅변대회에서 1등상을 탔어요.
3. 축하합니다!
4. 매우 감사합니다. 저는 운이 좋았어요.

LESSON 23(TWENTY-THREE)

BACK HOME 2

Mom, I'm back. Where's Mom?

She went to the supermarket.

When will she get back?

She's coming soon with some fruits.

NOTE

I'm back.: 돌아왔습니다.

She's coming soon.: 그녀는 곧 올 것이다.

with some fruits: 과일을 좀 가지고

USEFUL EXPRESSIONS 23

A: What's wrong with you? Does it hurt?
B: I fell down and hurt myself.

A: I always tell you to be careful.
B: Okay, give me some medicine.

NOTE

What's wrong with you? 무슨 일이야?(뭐 잘못된 것 있니?)
What's the matter with you? 무슨 일 있어?
Does it hurt? 다쳤니?
Are you in pain? 아프니?
Do you hurt your foot? 발을 다쳤니?
Give me some medicine. 약 좀 주세요.
I took some medicine. 나는 약을 먹었다.

★ 다음 글을 읽고 영어로 말하고 영어로 써 보세요.

1. 엄마, 다녀왔습니다. 엄마 어디 계셔?
2. 엄마 슈퍼마켓에 가셨어.
3. 언제 돌아오시니?
4. 과일을 좀 사 가지고 곧 돌아오실 거야.

1. 무슨 일이야? 다쳤어?
2. 넘어져서 다쳤어요.
3. 난 너에게 항상 주의하라고 말하잖아.
4. 알았어요. 약 좀 주세요.

LESSON 24(TWENTY-FOUR)

MIN-JAE'S ROOM

Clean your room, Min-jae.

Why? It's not dirty.

Whose books are these on the bed?

Those comic books aren't mine. They're Hyun-woo's.

NOTE

clean: 청소하다, 깨끗한
comic book: 만화책
comic: 만화의, 희극의
cartoon: 시사만화, 연재만화

USEFUL EXPRESSIONS 24

A: Is this your computer?
B: Yes, it is. My dad bought it for me on my birthday.

A: My dad promised to buy me a new one, too.
B: You're happy. Let's play computer games together in my room.

NOTE

4형식에서 간접목적어와 직접목적어의 위치를 서로 바꿀 때 간접목적어 앞에 전치사(to/for/of)를 넣으면 된다. 직접목적어가 명사면 바꿀 수 있지만 대명사면 4형식으로 표현할 수 없다.

예) My dad bought it for me. .... (O)
My dad bought me it. .... (X)
He gave me a book. .... (O)
He gave a book to me. .... (O)
He gave me it. .... (X)
He gave it to me. .... (O)

★ 다음 글을 읽고 영어로 말하고 영어로 써 보세요.

1. 민재야, 방 좀 치워라.
2. 왜요? 더럽지 않은데요.
3. 침대 위에 있는 이것들은 누구 책이니?
4. 그 만화책들은 제 것이 아니에요. 현우 것이에요.

1. 이것이 네 컴퓨터니?
2. 응, 그래. 아빠가 내 생일에 사주셨어.
3. 우리 아빠도 새 컴퓨터 사주시기로 약속하셨어.
4. 좋겠다. 내 방에서 컴퓨터 게임을 하자.

JI-MIN'S ROOM

NOTE

change one's clothes: 옷을 갈아입다

I have something to do now. 저는 지금 할 일이 있어요.

something to do: 할 일

(to do는 something을 꾸미는 형용사구이다.)

USEFUL EXPRESSIONS 25

A: Your room is clean and beautiful.
B: Thanks. Come and sit on the bed.

A: Who bought you this doll?
B: My mom did. I like it very much.

NOTE

Come and sit on the bed. 침대에 와서 앉아.
Who bought you this doll? 누가 이 인형을 사주셨니?
My mom did. 엄마가 사셨어.
did는 bought을 대신하는 대동사로 쓰였다.

★ 다음 글을 읽고 영어로 말하고 영어로 써 보세요.

1. 지민아, 샤워하고 옷을 갈아입어라.
2. 엄마, 잠깐만. 지금 할 일이 있어요.
3. 내가 백화점에서 네 새 블라우스를 하나 샀다.
4. 와! 금방 샤워할게요.

1. 네 방이 깨끗하고 아름답구나.
2. 고마워. 침대에 와서 앉아.
3. 누가 이 인형을 너에게 사주었니?
4. 엄마가 사주셨어. 난 이 인형이 무척 좋아.

LESSON 26(TWENTY-SIX)

MAKING DINNER

Give me some onions, Ji-min.

How many? Where are they?

Two. They're in the refrigerator.

Mom, here they are.

NOTE

How many? = How many onions?

Two. = Two onions.

refrigerator: 냉장고

ice box: 냉장고가 아니라 얼음통을 말한다.

USEFUL EXPRESSIONS 26

A: May I help you, Mom?
B: That'll be nice. I need some potatoes.

A: There aren't any potatoes in the basket.
B: Really? Would you go to the supermarket and buy some?

NOTE

onion: 양파
cucumber: 오이
potato: 감자
carrot: 당근
cabbage: 양배추
pumpkin: 호박
bean sprouts: 콩나물
spinach: 시금치
radish: 무
pepper: 후추
May I help you?: 도와드릴까요?(상대방의 의사를 묻는다.)
had better: ~하는 것이 좋겠다(명령의 우회적인 표현)

★ 다음 글을 읽고 영어로 말하고 영어로 써 보세요.

1. 지빈아, 양파 좀 줘.
2. 얼마나요? 어디에 있어요?
3. 2개. 냉장고 안에 있다.
4. 엄마, 여기 있어요.

1. 엄마, 제가 도와드릴까요?
2. 착하구나. 감자 몇 개 필요한데.
3. 바구니 안에 감자 하나도 없는데요.
4. 그러니? 슈퍼에 가서 몇 개 사다줄래?

LESSON 27(TWENTY-SEVEN)

THE DINNER TABLE

Your father isn't here yet.

Let's wait for Dad.

I'm hungry. Oh, dad is coming.

I'm sorry I'm late.

NOTE Your father isn't here yet.: 아빠가 아직 오시지 않았다.

I'm sorry I'm late.: 늦어서 미안하다.

USEFUL EXPRESSIONS 27

A: I invited an American friend today.
B: Really? What time? I have to prepare good food for dinner.

A: How about bulgogi?
B: That's a good idea. Most foreigners like it very much.

NOTE

Really? 그래요?
What time?: What time will he come?의 준말이다.
have to = must: ~해야 한다
for dinner: 정찬으로
식사 이름 앞에는 the를 붙이지 않는다.

★ 다음 글을 읽고 영어로 말하고 영어로 써 보세요.

1. 아빠가 아직 오시지 않았다.
2. 아빠를 기다리자.
3. 난 배고파. 아! 아빠가 오신다.
4. 늦어서 미안하다.

1. 나는 오늘 미국인 친구 한 사람을 초대했어요.
2. 정말이요? 몇 시에요? 만찬 준비를 해야겠네요.
3. 불고기는 어때요?
4. 그거 좋은 생각이에요. 대부분의 외국인들은 불고기를 무척 좋아해요.

IN THE LIVING ROOM 1

NOTE I didn't watch TV yesterday. 나는 어제 TV를 보지 않았다.

현재시제: I don't / You don't / He doesn't

과거시제: I didn't / You didn't / He didn't

USEFUL EXPRESSIONS 28

A: Turn off the TV, or you can't concentrate on your homework.
B: Let me watch the TV just a little longer.

A: No. Go upstairs and study, please.
B: You always tell me to study. Mom, I'm tired of that.

NOTE

turn off: 끄다(TV, 라디오, 전기스위치 등)
turn on: 켜다(TV, 라디오, 전기스위치 등)
concentrate on[upon]: ~에 집중을 하다
just a little longer: 조금만 더 오래
Study hard, or you can't go to college.
Study hard, and you can go to college.

★ 다음 글을 읽고 영어로 말하고 영어로 써 보세요.

1. 현우야, 너는 TV를 너무 많이 본다.
2. 엄마, 난 어제 TV를 보지 않았어요.
3. 우선 공부를 해라. 그러고 나서 TV를 봐도 된다.
4. 10분 후에 숙제를 할게요.

1. TV를 꺼라. 그렇지 않으면 너는 공부에 집중할 수 없다.
2. 조금 더 TV를 보게 해 주세요.
3. 안 돼. 2층으로 올라가 공부 좀 해라.
4. 엄마는 늘 저에게 공부하라고 하셨어요. 정말 지겨워요.

LESSON 29(TWENTY-NINE)

IN THE LIVING ROOM 2

NOTE

honey: 여보, 꿀

change the channel: 채널을 바꾸다

soap opera: 연속극

boxing match: 복싱 경기

USEFUL EXPRESSIONS 29

A: Hello, Min-jae please.
B: Hello, Min-jae speaking.

A: What are you doing?
B: I'm watching a boxing match on TV with my dad.

NOTE

Min–jae, please.	민재 좀 바꿔주세요.
May I speak to Min–jae?	민재 좀 바꿔주시겠어요?
Min–jae speaking.	민재인데요.
This is Min–jae speaking.	저 민재인데요.

on TV: TV에서
with my dad: 아빠와

★ 다음 글을 읽고 영어로 말하고 영어로 써 보세요.

1. 여보, 채널 좀 바꿔 줘요.
2. 안 돼요. 난 이 연속극이 좋아요.
3. 나는 권투 경기를 보고 싶은데.
4. 전 프로레슬링 경기를 보고 싶어요.

1. 여보세요, 민재 좀 바꿔주세요.
2. 여보세요, 민재인데요.
3. 뭐 하고 있니?
4. 아빠와 TV에서 권투 경기를 보고 있어.

LESSON 30(THIRTY)

GOING TO BED

It's time for your sleep.

I'm going to bed soon.

Go to bed after taking a shower.

Yes, Mom. Good night.

NOTE

for your sleep: 잠잘

go to bed(= sleep): 잠자리에 들다

I'm going to bed soon. 잠자리에 곧 들 예정이다.

I'll go to sleep soon. 곧 자러 갈게요.

USEFUL EXPRESSIONS 30

A: It's time to go to bed.
B: I'll go to sleep after reading a little more.

A: Reading some books is very good for all girls.
B: It's my hobby.

NOTE

It's time for your sleep. 네가 잠잘 시간이다.
It's time to go to bed. 잠자리에 들 시간이다.
동명사의 용법:
동명사는 명사처럼 전치사 뒤에 오거나 주어, 목적어, 보어 등으로 쓰인다.
1. 주어: Reading is good for us.
2. 목적어: I enjoy reading.
3. 보어: My hobby is reading.

★ 다음 글을 읽고 영어로 말하고 영어로 써 보세요.

1. 네가 잠잘 시간이야.
2. 곧 잘게요.
3. 샤워를 하고 자렴.
4. 예, 엄마. 안녕히 주무세요.

1. 잠자리에 들 시간이야.
2. 독서를 조금 더 하고 잘게요.
3. 책을 읽는 것은 모든 소녀에게 좋단다.
4. 그것(독서)이 제 취미예요.

LESSON 31(THIRTY-ONE)

SHOPPING 1

I'm going shopping this afternoon.

Then I'll come home as soon as possible.

What for?

Because I need a T-shirt.

NOTE

go shopping: 물건 사러 가다

as soon as possible: 될 수 있는 한 곧

What for(= Why?): 무엇 때문에? 왜?

USEFUL EXPRESSIONS 31

A: Mom, this T-shirt is very beautiful.
B: That's right. How much is it?

A: It's 50,000 won.
B: Wow! It's too expensive.

NOTE

go shopping: 물건 사러 가다
go fishing: 고기 잡으러 가다
go swimming: 수영하러 가다
go skating: 스케이트 타러 가다
go camping: 캠핑하러 가다
go hiking: 하이킹하러 가다

★ 다음 글을 읽고 영어로 말하고 영어로 써 보세요.

1. 오늘 오후 쇼핑하러 갈 예정이란다.
2. 그러면 될 수 있는 한 빨리 집에 올게요.
3. 뭣 때문에?
4. 왜냐하면 T셔츠가 하나 필요하거든요.

1. 엄마, 이 T셔츠는 매우 아름다워요.
2. 맞다. 얼마지?
3. 50,000원인데.
4. 와! 너무 비싼데요.

LESSON 32(THIRTY-TWO)

SHOPPING 2

Could you show me that blouse?

Here it is. This blouse is a new style.

Would you show me another one?

This one or that one?

NOTE Could[Would] you ~?의 구문은 상대방의 의사를 물어보는 공손한 표현이다.

Will[Can] you ~?의 구문은 상대방의 의사를 물어보는 보통의 표현이다.

This one or that one?은 Is it this one or that one?의 준말이다.

USEFUL EXPRESSIONS 32

A: That one, please.
B: Here you are.

A: Try it on. This blouse looks nice on you.
B: Thank you, Mom. I like it.

NOTE

this one: 이것(= this blouse: 이 블라우스)
that one: 저것(= that blouse: 저 블라우스)
Try it on: 입어봐
look nice on you: 너에게 잘 어울린다

Try it on.············(o)	Try the blouse on. ············(o)
Try on it.············(X)	Try on the blouse. ············(o)

★ 다음 글을 읽고 영어로 말하고 영어로 써 보세요.

1. 저 블라우스를 보여 주시겠어요?
2. 여기 있습니다. 이 블라우스는 새 스타일입니다.
3. 다른 것을 보여 주시겠습니까?
4. 이것이요? 저것이요?

1. 저것 좀 요.
2. 여기 있습니다.
3. 입어봐라. 이 블라우스는 너에게 잘 어울리는 구나.
4. 엄마, 고맙습니다. 난 이 블라우스가 좋아요.

LESSON 33(THIRTY-THREE)

SHOPPING 3

May I help you, ma'am?

No, thanks. Just looking.

How about this scarf?

That's nice. I'll buy you this one as a gift.

NOTE

May I help you? 어서 오십시오.(도와드릴까요?)

What can I do for you? 무엇을 도와드릴까요?

Just looking (around).: 그저 구경하고 있을 뿐이에요.

USEFUL EXPRESSIONS 33

A: Mom, I need a swimming suit for this summer.
B: O.K. I'll buy you one.

A: What else do you want?
B: A yellow beach ball and a red life jacket.

NOTE

swimming suit: 수영복
for this summer: 금년 여름에 쓸
what else: 그 밖에
a beach ball: 비치 볼
a life jacket: 구명조끼

★ 다음 글을 읽고 영어로 말하고 영어로 써 보세요.

1. 어서 오십시오, 아주머니.
2. 아니, 괜찮습니다. 그저 구경을 하고 있을 뿐이에요.
3. 이 스카프는 어때요?
4. 멋있습니다. 내가 당신에게 이것을 선물로 사 줄게요.

1. 엄마, 금년에 입을 수영복이 필요한데요.
2. 좋아, 내가 사 줄게.
3. 그 밖에 필요한 것은?
4. 노란색 비치 볼과 빨간색 구명조끼요.

SUMMER CAMP 1

leave for: ~으로 떠나다

camping trip: 캠핑 여행

the programs at the summer camp: summer camp의 프로그램

USEFUL EXPRESSIONS 34

A: Wow! Fantastic! It's wonderful!
B: Can we go swimming now?

A: Yes, of course. Be careful!
B: Don't worry. I can swim well.

NOTE

Fantastic!: 환상적이다!
wonderful: 놀라운, 아름다운
go swimming: 수영하러 가다
of course = sure = certainly: 물론
Be careful. = Take care of yourself.: 조심해라.

★ 다음 글을 읽고 영어로 말하고 영어로 써 보세요.

1. 몇 시에 우리는 캠핑을 떠나야 합니까?
2. 우리는 아침 8시에 떠나야 한다.
3. 여름 캠프의 프로그램을 저희에게 말씀해 주실 수 있어요?
4. 수영, 하이킹, 노래, 춤 그리고 캠프파이어야.

1. 와! 환상적이다! 너무 아름답다!
2. 지금 우리 수영해도 돼요?
3. 그럼, 물론. 조심해라.
4. 걱정 마세요. 전 수영을 잘해요.

LESSON 35(THIRTY-FIVE)

SUMMER CAMP 2

NOTE

warm up: 준비운동을 하다

warming-up: 준비운동의

Ready! Set! Go!: 준비! 마음을 가다듬고! 출발!

USEFUL EXPRESSIONS 35

A: I'm faster than you.
B: Right. You won the race.

A: I did it! I'm the fastest in my class.
B: Don't be too proud of yourself. Someday I'll beat you in the swimming race.

NOTE

I did it!: 나는 해냈다!(고생 끝에 어떤 일을 해냈을 때)
be proud of: ~을 자랑스럽게 여기다
I'll beat you.: 박살을 내다(이기다).
I'm faster than you. 나는 너보다 더 빠르다.
* 비교급 + than: ~보다 더
the + 최상급 + in: ~에서 가장 …하다

★ 다음 글을 읽고 영어로 말하고 영어로 써 보세요.

1. 네 수영복이 아주 아름답구나. 너 수영 잘할 수 있니?
2. 고마워. 그럼, 물론이지. 나는 수영을 아주 잘할 수 있어.
3. 나도 잘해! 수영 시합하는 것 어때?
4. 좋아. 우린 준비운동을 할 필요가 있어. 준비! 마음을 가다듬고! 출발!

1. 나는 너보다 더 빨라.
2. 맞아. 네가 시합에서 이겼다.
3. 나는 해냈어! 나는 우리 반에서 가장 빨라.
4. 자랑하지 마. 언젠가는 수영에서 너를 이기고 말 거야.

LESSON 36(THIRTY-SIX)

WINTER VACATION

When is your winter vacation?

From December 21st to February 5th. It is 45 days long.

Our winter vacation is very short. It's only for two weeks.

It's very short, isn't it?

NOTE

from December 21st to February 5th: 12월 21일부터 2월 5일까지

It is 45 days long.: 45일간이다.

only for two weeks: 단 2주간

USEFUL EXPRESSIONS 36

A: What are you going to do during the winter vacation?
B: I'm going skiing.

A: With whom and where?
B: With my family and at Yong Pyeong Ski Resort.

부가의문문: 상대방에게 동의나 확인을 얻기 위해서 쓰는 표현이다.
You have a short winter vacation, don't you?
You don't have a short winter vacation, do you?
He goes skiing, doesn't he?
He doesn't go skiing, does he?
It's fine today, isn't it?
It's not fine today, is it?

★ 다음 글을 읽고 영어로 말하고 영어로 써 보세요.

1. 너의 겨울방학은 언제니?
2. 12월 21일부터 2월 5일까지야. 45일간이야.
3. 우리 겨울방학은 매우 짧아. 겨우 2주간이야.
4. 정말 짧구나.

1. 너는 겨울방학 동안에 무엇을 할 예정이니?
2. 나는 스키를 타러 갈 거야.
3. 누구와 어디에?
4. 나의 가족과 용평 스키장에.

LESSON 37(THIRTY-SEVEN)

JI-MIN'S BIRTHDAY

Happy birthday, Ji-min.

Thank you, come in.
Su-jin is already here.

This is for you.

Thank you for coming
to my birthday party.

NOTE

Happy birthday, Ji-min. 지민아, 생일 축하해.

This is for you. 이것이 너에게 줄 거야.

Thank you for coming. 와 주어서 고마워.

A: Dad, what will you buy me as a birthday gift?
B: You told me you wanted an audio set, Ji-min.

A: Yes, I did. Can you, Dad?
B: Sure, I will.

NOTE

as a birthday gift: 생일선물로(as: ~으로)
You told me (that) you wanted an audio set.
that 이하는 명사절로 that을 생략할 수 있다.
Can you? = Can you buy me a gift?
Sure, I will. 물론, 내가 사 줄게.

★ 다음 글을 읽고 영어로 말하고 영어로 써 보세요.

1. 지민아, 생일 축하해.
2. 고마워, 들어와. 수진이가 벌써 여기에 와 있어.
3. 이것은 너에게 줄 거야.
4. 내 생일파티에 와 주어서 고마워.

1. 아빠, 생일선물로 저에게 무엇을 사 주실 거예요?
2. 지민아, 넌 오디오 세트를 가지고 싶다고 나에게 말했지.
3. 예, 그랬어요. 아빠 사 주실 수 있어요?
4. 물론, 내가 사 줄게.

LESSON 38(THIRTY-EIGHT)

AN AMERICAN FRIEND'S VISIT

This is my American friend's daughter.

Hi, I'm Min-jae.

Hello, my name is Jane. Glad to meet you.

Nice to meet you, too.

This is Jane. 이 애가 제인이다.

Glad to meet you. 만나서 반가워.

Nice to meet you, too. 역시 만나서 반가워.

American friend's daughter: 미국인 친구의 딸

USEFUL EXPRESSIONS 38

A: How long will you stay in Seoul?
B: I'll stay here for a week. I'm on the summer vacation.

A: I'll be a guide for you if you want.
B: Thank you. I'd like to take a tour of the city.

NOTE

on the summer vacation: 여름방학 중
I'll be a guide for you.: 너를 위해서 가이드가 되겠다.
if you want: 만일 당신이 원한다면
I'd like to: ~하고 싶다
take a tour: 관광 여행하다

★ 다음 글을 읽고 영어로 말하고 영어로 써 보세요.

1. 이 애가 나의 미국인 친구의 딸이다.
2. 안녕, 내가 민재야.
3. 안녕, 내 이름은 제인이야. 만나서 반가워.
4. 역시 만나서 반가워.

1. 서울에 얼마 동안 있을 거니?
2. 1주일 동안 머물 거야. 나는 여름방학 중이야.
3. 네가 원한다면 내가 너를 위해 가이드가 되어 줄게.
4. 고마워. 시내 관광을 하고 싶어.

LESSON 39(THIRTY-NINE)

TAKING A TOUR

Are there any good places of interest for me to visit?

Certainly! Seorak Mountain, Gyeongju, Jeju Island and so on.

Can you recommend a good place of interest for a week?

Sure! Gyeongju is the best place to visit.

a good place of interest: 관광명소

and so on(= and so forth): 등등, 따위

the best place to visit: 가 볼만한 가장 좋은 곳

USEFUL EXPRESSIONS 39

A: Gyeongju is a Korean historical site that is ten centuries old.
B: Really? How long does it take from Seoul to get there?

A: It takes about four hours to get there by express bus.
B: I'd like to visit there.

NOTE

a Korean historical site: 한국의 역사 고적지
ten centuries: 10세기, 1,000년
Really?: 정말? 그래?(어떤 말을 듣고 놀라는 표현이다.)
by express bus: 고속버스로
It takes about four hours to get there. 그곳에 가는 데 4시간 걸린다.
it은 비인칭 주어로 시간, 거리, 날씨, 명암 등을 나타낸다.

★ 다음 글을 읽고 영어로 말하고 영어로 써 보세요.

1. 내가 가 볼만한 훌륭한 곳이 있니?
2. 물론이지! 설악산, 경주, 제주도 등이야.
3. 너 1주일 동안 갈 수 있는 관광명소를 추천할 수 있니?
4. 물론이지. 경주가 가 볼만한 최고의 명소야.

1. 경주는 1,000년이나 된 한국의 역사적인 명소야.
2. 정말? 서울에서 거기에 가는 데 얼마나 걸리니?
3. 고속버스로 약 4시간 걸려.
4. 나는 거기에 가고 싶어.

LESSON 40(FORTY)

TELEPHONE 1

Hello! May I speak to Ji-min?

This is Ji-min speaking.

Hi, Ji-min. How are you?

I don't feel very good.

NOTE May I speak to Ji-min? 지민이 좀 바꿔 주시겠어요?

This is Ji-min (speaking). 제가 지민인데요.

I don't feel very good. 기분이 아주 좋지는 않아요.

USEFUL EXPRESSIONS 40

A: Hello! May I speak to Jane?
B: Who's calling, please?

A: This is Min-jae.
B: Just a moment, please.

NOTE

May I speak to Jane?	제인 좀 바꿔 주시겠어요?
Can I talk to Jane?	제인 좀 바꿔 주실 수 있어요?
I'd like to speak to Jane.	제인 좀 바꿔 주세요.
Who's calling, please?	누구시지요?
May I ask who's calling?	누구시지요?
Who is this, please?	누구시지요?

★ 다음 글을 읽고 영어로 말하고 영어로 써 보세요.

1. 여보세요? 지민이 좀 바꿔 주시겠어요?
2. 제가 지민인데요.
3. 안녕, 지민. 어떻게 지내니?
4. 기분이 아주 좋지는 않아.

1. 여보세요! 제인 좀 바꿔 주시겠어요?
2. 누구시지요?
3. 저 민재인데요.
4. 잠깐 기다리세요.

LESSON 41(FORTY-ONE)

TELEPHONE 2

Hello! This is Jane. I'd like to speak to Ji-min.

She's not at home now.

What time is she expected back?

In about an hour.

NOTE

She's not at home now. 지금 집에 없는데.

What time is she expected (to be) back? 몇 시에 돌아올까요?

In about an hour: 1시간 후에

USEFUL EXPRESSIONS 41

A: Hello. Is this 855-6343?
B: Yes, it is.

A: May I speak to Miss Bang?
B: She has just gone out.

NOTE

Just a moment, please.	잠깐만 기다려 주세요.
Just a minute, please.	잠깐만 기다려 주세요.
One moment, please.	잠깐만 기다려 주세요.
Hold on, please.	잠깐만 기다려 주세요.
May I take a message?	메시지를 남기시겠어요?
I'd like to leave a message.	메시지를 남기고 싶은데요.

★ 다음 글을 읽고 영어로 말하고 영어로 써 보세요.

1. 여보세요? 제인인데요. 지민이 좀 바꿔 주세요.
2. 지금 지민이 집에 없는데.
3. 몇 시에 돌아올 것 같아요?
4. 약 1시간 후에.

1. 여보세요. 855-6343이지요?
2. 예, 그렇습니다.
3. 방 선생님 좀 바꿔 주시겠어요?
4. 금방 나갔는데요.

LESSON 42(FORTY-TWO)

TELEPHONE 3

Hello! May I speak to Mr. Bang?

He's talking on another line.

접수처

O.K. I'll call again.

Call again in ten minutes, please.

NOTE

He's talking on another line. 다른 전화를 받고 계십니다.

I'll call again. 다시 걸게요.

Call again in ten minutes, please. 10분 후에 다시 걸어 주세요.

USEFUL EXPRESSIONS 42

A: Is this Bansok Foreign Language Institute?
B: No. You have the wrong number.

A: What number did you dial?
B: I dialed 856-6343.

NOTE

You have the wrong number.	전화 잘못 거셨습니다.
I've dialed the wrong number.	전화를 잘못 걸었습니다.
Who's calling, please?	누구시지요?
Who's this calling, please?	누구시지요?
Who are you calling?	누구에게 전화를 거셨습니까?
I'll call you back.	다시 전화하겠습니다.

★ 다음 글을 읽고 영어로 말하고 영어로 써 보세요.

1. 여보세요! 방 선생님 바꿔 주시겠어요?
2. 다른 전화를 받고 계십니다.
3. 알았습니다. 제가 다시 걸겠습니다.
4. 10분 후에 다시 걸어 주십시오.

1. 반석 외국어 학원이지요?
2. 아니오, 전화 잘못 거셨습니다.
3. 몇 번 거셨지요?
4. 856-6343 걸었습니다.

LESSON 43(FORTY-THREE)

TELEPHONE 4

Hello, may I speak to Min-ji?

Who's calling, please?

This is Min-ji's friend, Min-jae. How are you?

Just a minute. Min-ji,... telephone.

NOTE

Min-ji, telephone. 민지야, 전화.

Min-ji, your phone. 민지야, 네 전화.

Min-ji's friend, Min-jae 민지 친구, 민재

USEFUL EXPRESSIONS 43

A: Hello, this is Min-ji speaking.
B: Min-jae speaking. Hi, Min-ji. Are you free tomorrow?

A: Yes, I'm free. What's up?
B: How about meeting at Sillim Subway Station at noon?

NOTE

This is Min–ji speaking.	제가 민지인데요.
This is Min–ji.	제가 민지인데요.
Min–ji speaking.	민지인데요.
This is she.	전데요.
That's me.	전데요.
What's up?	무슨 일인데?

★ 다음 글을 읽고 영어로 말하고 영어로 써 보세요.

1. 여보세요. 민지 좀 바꿔 주시겠어요?
2. 누구시지요?
3. 민지 친구 민재인데요. 안녕하세요?
4. 잠깐만. 민지야... 전화.

1. 여보세요. 저 민지인데요.
2. 민재야. 안녕, 민지. 내일 시간 있니?
3. 응, 시간 있어. 무슨 일이야?
4. 정오에 신림 전철역에서 만나는 거 어때?

LESSON 44(FORTY-FOUR)

TELEPHONE 5

What's the telephone number of Bansok Foreign Language School?

Just a moment, please.

The number is 2093-3399.

Thank you, information.

NOTE That number is 2093-3399. 2093-3399입니다.

전화번호를 말할 때 that으로 표현한다.

전화를 받을 때 this로 표현한다.

USEFUL EXPRESSIONS 44

A: Hello. I'd like to speak to Mr. Kim.
B: I'm sorry. You must have the wrong number. There's no one here by that name.

A: I'm sorry.
B: That's all right.

NOTE

You must have the wrong number.	전화 잘못 거셨습니다.
There's no one here by that name.	그런 사람 없는데요.
The line is busy.	통화중입니다.
Sorry, he's still on the line.	죄송합니다만, 아직도 통화중인데요.
He's out now.	그는 지금 외출 중인데요.
He's off duty today.	그는 오늘 쉽니다.

★ 다음 글을 읽고 영어로 말하고 영어로 써 보세요.

1. 반석 외국어 학교 전화번호가 몇 번입니까?
2. 잠깐 기다리세요.
3. 전화번호가 2093-3399입니다.
4. 안내, 고맙습니다.

1. 여보세요. 김 선생님 바꿔 주세요.
2. 미안합니다. 전화 잘못 거셨습니다. 그런 이름 가진 사람은 없는데요.
3. 미안합니다.
4. 괜찮습니다.

CLASSROOM ENGLISH

MEMO

CLASSROOM ENGLISH 1

S Good morning, sir.

T Good morning, class. How are you this morning?

S We are just fine. Thank you. And you?

T Fine, thanks. Stop talking, Ji-hoon.

S I'm sorry.

T Did you do your homework?

S Yes, we did.

T Hand in your homework.

S Here it is.

T You are good students.

교실 영어 1

영어로 말하고 영어로 써 보세요. (영어로 읽기 소요시간: 20초 이내)

S 선생님, 안녕하세요.

T 여러분, 안녕하세요. 오늘 아침은 어때요?

S 좋아요, 고맙습니다. 선생님은 어떠세요?

T 좋아요, 고마워요. 조용히 해라, 지훈아.

S 죄송합니다.

T 너희들 숙제해왔니?

S 예, 했어요.

T 숙제를 내 보렴.

S 여기 있어요.

T 너희들은 착한 학생이로구나.

CLASSROOM ENGLISH 2

T Hello, everyone.

S Good morning, sir.

T Before class, let me call the roll. Is there anyone absent today?

S Su-hee is absent, sir.

T Do you know why Su-hee is absent today?

S I called her today, and her mother told me she is sick in bed with a cold.

T Oh, Su-hee is coming now. Are you all right?

S No, I'm not. I have a fever.

교실 영어 2

영어로 말하고 영어로 써 보세요. (영어로 읽기 소요시간: 25초 이내) 

T 여러분, 안녕.

S 선생님, 안녕하세요.

T 수업 전에, 출석을 부르겠어요. 오늘 결석한 학생 있어요?

S 선생님, 수희가 결석했어요.

T 오늘 수희가 왜 결석했는지 아는 학생 있어요?

S 오늘 수희에게 전화했는데요. 감기 때문에 아파서 누워 있다고 수희 어머니가 말씀하셨어요.

T 지금 수희가 오고 있구나. 괜찮니?

S 아니오, 열이 좀 있어요.

CLASSROOM ENGLISH 3

T Good afternoon, class.

S Good afternoon, sir.

T Where are we today?

S We are on Lesson 7, page 18, sir.

T Is there anyone who would like to read this lesson?

S I would sir.

T Min-jae, speak up, please. I can't hear you.

S Yes, sir.

T Good. Listen and repeat.

교실 영어 3

영어로 말하고 영어로 써 보세요. (영어로 읽기 소요시간: 20초 이내)

T 여러분, 안녕하세요.

S 선생님, 안녕하세요.

T 오늘 수업 어디서부터 시작되죠?

S 7과 18페이지입니다, 선생님.

T 이 과를 읽을 사람 있어요?

S 제가 읽겠어요, 선생님.

T 민재야, 크게 읽어. 안 들려요.

S 예, 선생님.

T 좋아, 잘 듣고 따라 읽으세요.

CLASSROOM ENGLISH 4

T Hi, everybody.

S Good morning, ma'am.

T Who is it?

S It's me, Ji-min.

T Come in. Why are you late for this class?

S I'm sorry I'm late. I overslept this morning.

T I'll punish you if you are late again.

S Yes, ma'am.

T Go to your seat and sit down.

S Thank you, ma'am.

교실 영어 4 영어로 말하고 영어로 써 보세요. (영어로 읽기 소요시간: 20초 이내)

T 여러분, 안녕.

S 선생님, 안녕하세요.

T 누구야?

S 저 지민이에요.

T 들어와요. 너 수업에 왜 늦었니?

S 늦어서 죄송합니다. 오늘 아침 늦잠 잤어요.

T 너 또 늦으면 벌을 주겠어요.

S 예, 선생님.

T 네 자리에 가서 앉아라.

S 감사합니다, 선생님.

CLASSROOM ENGLISH 5

T Do you have any questions?

S Me, me, me.

T O.K. Hyun-woo, go ahead.

S I can't understand the point of infinitive.

T O.K. I'll explain the point of infinitive once more. Got it?

S Yes, I got it.

T Are there any questions?

S No, there aren't any.

T O.K. Time is up. See you tomorrow.

S Thank you, sir. Good-bye.

교실 영어 5

영어로 말하고 영어로 써 보세요. (영어로 읽기 소요시간: 22초 이내)

T 질문 있어요?

S 저요, 저요, 저요.

T 좋아, 현우야. 자 질문해 봐.

S 전 부정사의 요점을 이해할 수 없어요.

T 좋아, 한 번 더 부정사의 요점을 설명할게. 알겠니?

S 예, 알겠어요.

T 질문 또 있니?

S 아뇨, 없어요.

T 좋아, 시간이 다 됐다. 내일 보자.

S 선생님, 감사합니다. 안녕히 가세요.

CLASSROOM ENGLISH 6

T We have a short test today.
S Oh, ma'am. That's too often.

T But it's for your benefit.
S We're tired of that.

T Be quiet! Okay, clean your desks. Take out a clean sheet of paper and a pencil only.

T I'll read each question to you. Please listen carefully and write your answers.

T Please raise your right hand if you need to hear the question again. Don't forget to write your name on the right hand corner.

T Is everyone ready? Let's begin.

교실 영어 6 영어로 말하고 영어로 써 보세요. (영어로 읽기 소요시간: 34초 이내)

T 오늘 여러분 쪽지시험을 볼게요.

S 오, 선생님. 시험을 너무 자주 봐요.

T 하지만 시험은 너희들을 위해서예요.

S 우린 시험에 질렸어요.

T 조용히 해요! 좋아, 책상을 깨끗이 치워요. 깨끗한 종이 한 장과 연필 한 자루만을 꺼내요.

T 여러분에게 문제 하나하나를 읽어 줄게요. 잘 듣고 답을 써요.

T 여러분이 문제를 다시 한 번 듣고 싶으면 오른손을 들어요. 오른쪽 귀퉁이에 이름 쓰는 것을 잊지 말아요.

T 모두 준비됐지? 시작하자.

CLASSROOM ENGLISH 7

T Keep your eyes on your own paper.

S Yes, ma'am.

T If you look on someone else's paper, you will get an automatic zero.

S Yes, ma'am.

T If you don't know the answer, skip it. Then go on to the next.

S Yes, ma'am.

T O.K. It's time to finish.

S Ma'am, wait for a few minutes, please.

T No, you had enough time to write your answers.

S Yes, ma'am.

T Please pass your papers to the front.

S Yes, ma'am. Thank you. Good-bye.

교실 영어 7

영어로 말하고 영어로 써 보세요. (영어로 읽기 소요시간: 32초 이내)

T 네 시험지에서 눈을 떼지 마라.

S 예, 선생님.

T 만일 다른 사람의 시험지를 보면 너희들은 자동적으로 빵점 처리될 거예요.

S 예, 선생님.

T 만일 답을 모르면 건너뛰어요. 그러고 나서 다음 문제를 계속 풀어요.

S 예, 선생님.

T 좋아. 이제 끝낼 시간이에요.

S 선생님, 잠시만 기다려 주세요.

T 안 돼요. 너희들이 답을 쓸 시간은 충분했어요.

S 예, 선생님.

T 너희들 시험지를 앞으로 보내세요.

S 예, 선생님. 고맙습니다. 안녕히 가세요.

Lesson 1 p. 8

★ 다음 글을 읽고 영어로 말하고 영어로 써 보세요.

I. 1. Wake up, Ji-min.
2. Okay, Mom.
3. Good morning, Ji-min.
4. Good morning, Mom.

II. 1. Wake up, wake up, Min-jae.
2. I'm sleepy, Mom.
3. We're going on a picnic to the Seoul Grand Park today.
4. I'm up already.

Lesson 2 p. 10

★ 다음 글을 읽고 영어로 말하고 영어로 써 보세요.

I. 1. Wake up, Hyun-woo.
2. Dad is waiting for you in the garden.
3. O.K. I'll wear my sweat pants and go out.
4. Hurry up, Hyun-woo. I'm ready. Let's run.

II. 1. Hiking is good for the health.
2. Jogging is good for the health, too.
3. Doing exercise is good for us.
4. Exercising every day is not easy.

Lesson 3 p. 12

★ 다음 글을 읽고 영어로 말하고 영어로 써 보세요.

I. 1. Wash your face and brush your teeth.
2. All right.
3. Your towel.
4. Thanks, Mom.

II. 1. Did you wash your hair?
2. No, I didn't.
3. Don't forget to wash your hair every day.
4. Yes, Mom.

Lesson 4 p. 14

★ 다음 글을 읽고 영어로 말하고 영어로 써 보세요.

I. 1. What are you doing?
2. I'm taking a shower.
3. What? I have to pee right now.
4. Wait a minute.

II. 1. Come out quickly.
2. All right. I'm trying.
3. You're always in the bathroom for a long time.
4. How about you?

Lesson 5 p. 16

★ 다음 글을 읽고 영어로 말하고 영어로 써 보세요.

I. 1. The breakfast is ready.
2. Is that my toast?
3. Yes, it is. It's for you.
4. Pass that to me.

II. 1. Do you like this hamburger?
2. Yes, I do. It tastes good.
3. More please.
4. No. You'll get a stomachache.

Lesson 6 p. 18

★ 다음 글을 읽고 영어로 말하고 영어로 써 보세요.

I. 1. This bean paste soup is delicious.
2. Thank you.
3. Give me some more, please.

4. All right, but only a little more.

II. 1. This pizza tastes very good.

2. Do you want another slice?

3. No, thank you. I'm full.

4. You're right. It's not good to eat too much.

Lesson 7 p. 20

★ 다음 글을 읽고 영어로 말하고 영어로 써 보세요.

I. 1. May I have some more rice?

2. All right. Hand me your bowl.

3. Thank you, Mom.

4. Don't eat too fast. Take your time.

II. 1. Would you like some meat?

2. Give me a little.

3. Do you want some bread?

4. Yes. put some jam on it, please.

Lesson 8 p. 22

★ 다음 글을 읽고 영어로 말하고 영어로 써 보세요.

I. 1. Would you like some coffee?

2. Of course, a cup of coffee, please.

3. Here you are.

4. Thank you.

II. 1. Ice cream or fruit for dessert?

2. Fruit, please.

3. What kind of fruit do you like?

4. I like grapes.

Lesson 9 p. 24

★ 다음 글을 읽고 영어로 말하고 영어로 써 보세요.

I. 1. It's raining now.

2. Where's my umbrella?

3. It's in the basket at the entrance.

4. Okay, I found it.

II. 1. It is cold today.

2. I'll wear the sweater.

3. Watch out on the ice.

4. Don't worry.

Lesson 10 p. 26

★ 다음 글을 읽고 영어로 말하고 영어로 써 보세요.

I. 1. Hurry up, Ji-min.

2. What time is it now?

3. It's eight.

4. I must hurry to school.

II. 1. When are you coming home?

2. About four.

3. What out for cars.

4. All right, don't worry about me.

Lesson 11 p. 28

★ 다음 글을 읽고 영어로 말하고 영어로 써 보세요.

I. 1. Hi.

2. Hello. How are you?

3. Fine, thank you. And you?

4. I'm fine, thank you.

II. 1. How are you this morning?

2. I'm fine, thanks. And how are you?

3. I'm fine, too.

4. Let's go to school quickly.

Lesson 12 p. 30

★ 다음 글을 읽고 영어로 말하고 영어로 써 보세요.

I. 1. Hello, Mi-ae.

2. Hi, Ji-min.

3. We're late for school this morning.

4. That's right. Let's run to school.

II. 1. We're late today.

2. How about taking a bus?

3. That's a good idea.
4. A bus is coming here.

Lesson 13 p. 32

★ 다음 글을 읽고 영어로 말하고 영어로 써 보세요.

I. 1. Good morning, class.
2. Good morning, sir.
3. Let's start our class.
4. Yes, sir. It's Lesson 5.

II. 1. Open your books to page 15.
2. Yes, ma'am.
3. Did you do your homework?
4. Yes, we did.

Lesson 14 p. 34

★ 다음 글을 읽고 영어로 말하고 영어로 써 보세요.

I. 1. Stop talking, Hyun-woo. Look at me.
2. I'm sorry, ma'am.
3. Read at the beginning of Lesson 5.
4. Lesson 5. The breakfast is ready.

II. 1. Be quiet, everyone. Hyun-woo, speak up.
2. Yes, ma'am.
3. Good. You're a good reader.
4. Thank you, ma'am.

Lesson 15 p. 36

★ 다음 글을 읽고 영어로 말하고 영어로 써 보세요.

I. 1. It's time to have lunch.
2. Let me see your food tray.
3. Wow! Your lunch looks very delicious.
4. Thanks. Today is my birthday.

II. 1. Let's have lunch with me.
2. O.K. I'll bring some water.
3. Thank you. I want cold water.
4. Here it is.

Lesson 16 p. 38

★ 다음 글을 읽고 영어로 말하고 영어로 써 보세요.

I. 1. What is for lunch today?
2. Well, I don't know. Let's hurry to the cafeteria.
3. Sandwiches and apples.
4. Let's eat quickly and go out.

II. 1. Which food do you like better?
2. I like pizza better than hamburger.
3. Pizza is more expensive than hamburger.
4. Don't worry. I have some money to buy pizza.

Lesson 17 p. 40

★ 다음 글을 읽고 영어로 말하고 영어로 써 보세요.

I. 1. Let's play hide-and-seek.
2. That's a good idea. I'll gather friends.
3. I want to be a tagger.
4. O.K. Ready go.

II. 1. How about leapfrog?
2. Okay, good.
3. You are too heavy.
4. Don't worry. I'm on a diet.

Lesson 18 p. 42

★ 다음 글을 읽고 영어로 말하고 영어로 써 보세요.

I. 1. Did you bring a skipping rope?
2. Yes, I brought it. Let's skip.
3. Can you skip well?

4. Yes, I can. Of course. I can skip better than any other girls.

II. 1. How about a game with a ball?
2. All right.
3. Let's play dodgeball.
4. The bell is ringing. Let's go into the classroom quickly.

Lesson 19 p. 44

★ 다음 글을 읽고 영어로 말하고 영어로 써 보세요.

I. 1. I don't like math. It's difficult for me.
2. Me, neither. I like social studies better.
3. Stop talking, Ji-min and Mi-ae.
4. I'm sorry. I'll be quiet.

II. 1. I like science. I want to be a scientist.
2. Me, too.
3. My dad bought me a computer on my birthday.
4. Let's go to my home and play computer games.

Lesson 20 p. 46

★ 다음 글을 읽고 영어로 말하고 영어로 써 보세요.

I. 1. Let's play basketball.
2. Sorry. I have to do my homework.
3. Let's do our homework later.
4. All right. Let's play for only an hour.

II. 1. How about going to a basketball game?
2. That's a good idea.
3. I like Huh-hoon, the best basketball player.
4. That's right. He is this season's basketball MVP.

Lesson 21 p. 48

★ 다음 글을 읽고 영어로 말하고 영어로 써 보세요.

I. 1. Let's go and get some ice cream.
2. What kind of ice cream do you like?
3. I like strawberry ice cream.
4. I want to have vanilla and chocolate icecream.

II. 1. I'm hungry. How about tteokbokki?
2. That's good. Tteokbokki is my favorite food.
3. Don't eat too fast. There are only a few on the plate.
4. O.K., but you, too.

Lesson 22 p. 50

★ 다음 글을 읽고 영어로 말하고 영어로 써 보세요.

I. 1. I'm home, Mom.
2. Come on in. Are you hungry?
3. Yes, Mom. I'm very hungry.
4. Here is some pizza you like.

II. 1. How's your English Speech Contest?
2. I got a first prize at the English Speech Contest.
3. Congratulations!
4. Thank you very much. I'm lucky.

Lesson 23 p. 52

★ 다음 글을 읽고 영어로 말하고 영어로 써 보세요.

I. 1. Mom, I'm back. Where's Mom?
2. She went to the supermarket.
3. When will she get back?
4. She's coming soon with some fruits.

II. 1. What's wrong with you? Does it

hurt?

2. I fell down and hurt myself.
3. I always tell you to be careful.
4. Okay, give me some medicine.

Lesson 24 p. 54

★ 다음 글을 읽고 영어로 말하고 영어로 써 보세요.

I. 1. Clean your room, Min-jae.
2. Why? It's not dirty.
3. Whose books are these on the bed?
4. Those comic books aren't mine. They're Hyun-woo's.

II. 1. Is this your computer?
2. Yes, it is. My dad bought it for me on my birthday.
3. My dad promised to buy me a new one, too.
4. You're happy. Let's play computer games together in my room.

Lesson 25 p. 56

★ 다음 글을 읽고 영어로 말하고 영어로 써 보세요.

I. 1. Ji-min, take a shower and change your clothes.
2. Wait a minute, Mom. I have something to do now.
3. I bought your new blouse at the department store.
4. Wow! I'll take a shower soon.

II. 1. Your room is clean and beautiful.
2. Thanks. Come and sit on the bed.
3. Who bought you this doll?
4. My mom did. I like it very much.

Lesson 26 p. 58

★ 다음 글을 읽고 영어로 말하고 영어로 써 보세요.

I. 1. Give me some onions, Ji-min.
2. How many? Where are they?
3. Two. They're in the refrigerator.
4. Mom, here they are.

II. 1. May I help you, Mom?
2. That'll be nice. I need some potatoes.
3. There aren't any potatoes in the basket.
4. Really? Would you go to the supermarket and buy some?

Lesson 27 p. 60

★ 다음 글을 읽고 영어로 말하고 영어로 써 보세요.

I. 1. Your father isn't here yet.
2. Let's wait for Dad.
3. I'm hungry. Oh, dad is coming.
4. I'm sorry I'm late.

II. 1. I invited an American friend today.
2. Really? What time? I have to prepare good food for dinner.
3. How about bulgogi?
4. That's a good idea. Most foreigners like it very much.

Lesson 28 p.62

★ 다음 글을 읽고 영어로 말하고 영어로 써 보세요.

I. 1. Hyun-woo, you watch too much TV.
2. Mom, I didn't watch TV yesterday.
3. Study first. And then you can watch it later.
4. After ten minutes, I'll do my homework.

II. 1. Turn off the TV, or you can't concentrate on your homework.
2. Let me watch the TV just a little

longer.

3. No. Go upstairs and study, please.
4. You always tell me to study. Mom, I'm tired of that.

Lesson 29 p. 64

★ 다음 글을 읽고 영어로 말하고 영어로 써 보세요.

I. 1. Honey, change the channel, please.
2. No, I like this soap opera.
3. I want to watch a boxing match.
4. I'd like to watch a pro wrestling match.

II. 1. Hello, Min-jae please.
2. Hello, Min-jae speaking.
3. What are you doing?
4. I'm watching a boxing match on TV with my dad.

Lesson 30 p. 66

★ 다음 글을 읽고 영어로 말하고 영어로 써 보세요.

I. 1. It's time for your sleep.
2. I'm going to bed soon.
3. Go to bed after taking a shower.
4. Yes, Mom. Good night.

II. 1. It's time to go to bed.
2. I'll go to sleep after reading a little more.
3. Reading some books is very good for all girls.
4. It's my hobby.

Lesson 31 p. 68

★ 다음 글을 읽고 영어로 말하고 영어로 써 보세요.

I. 1. I'm going shopping this afternoon.
2. Then I'll come home as soon as possible.
3. What for?
4. Because I need a T-shirt.

II. 1. Mom, this T-shirt is very beautiful.
2. That's right. How much is it?
3. It's 50,000 won.
4. Wow! It's too expensive.

Lesson 32 p. 70

★ 다음 글을 읽고 영어로 말하고 영어로 써 보세요.

I. 1. Could you show me that blouse?
2. Here it is. This blouse is a new style.
3. Would you show me another one?
4. This one or that one?

II. 1. That one, please.
2. Here you are.
3. Try it on. This blouse looks nice on you.
4. Thank you, Mom. I like it.

Lesson 33 p. 72

★ 다음 글을 읽고 영어로 말하고 영어로 써 보세요.

I. 1. May I help you, ma'am?
2. No, thanks. Just looking.
3. How about this scarf?
4. That's nice. I'll buy you this one as a gift.

II. 1. Mom, I need a swimming suit for this summer.
2. O.K. I'll buy you one.
3. What else do you want?
4. A yellow beach ball and a red life jacket.

Lesson 34 p. 74

★ 다음 글을 읽고 영어로 말하고 영어로 써 보세요.

I. 1. What time should we leave for our camping trip?
2. We should leave at eight in the morning.
3. Could you tell us the programs at the summer camp?
4. Swimming, hiking, singing, dancing, and camp fire.

II. 1. Wow! Fantastic! It's wonderful!
2. Can we go swimming now?
3. Yes, of course. Be careful!
4. Don't worry. I can swim well.

Lesson 35 p. 76

★ 다음 글을 읽고 영어로 말하고 영어로 써 보세요.

I. 1. Your swimming suit is so beautiful. Can you swim well?
2. Thanks. Yes, of course. I can swim very well.
3. Me, too! How about swimming race?
4. Okay. We need to warm up. Ready! Set! Go!

II. 1. I'm faster than you.
2. Right. You won the race.
3. I did it! I'm the fastest in my class.
4. Don't be too proud of yourself. Someday I'll beat you in the swimming race.

Lesson 36 p. 78

★ 다음 글을 읽고 영어로 말하고 영어로 써 보세요.

I. 1. When is your winter vacation?
2. From December 21st to February 5th. It is 45 days long.
3. Our winter vacation is very short. It's only for two weeks.
4. It's very short, isn't it?

II. 1. What are you going to do during the winter vacation?
2. I'm going skiing.
3. With whom and where?
4. With my family and at Yong Pyeong Ski Resort.

Lesson 37 p. 80

★ 다음 글을 읽고 영어로 말하고 영어로 써 보세요.

I. 1. Happy birthday, Ji-min.
2. Thank you, come in. Su-jin is already here.
3. This is for you.
4. Thank you for coming to my birthday party.

II. 1. Dad, what will you buy me as a birthday gift?
2. You told me you wanted an audio set, Ji-min.
3. Yes, I did. Can you, Dad?
4. Sure, I will.

Lesson 38 p. 82

★ 다음 글을 읽고 영어로 말하고 영어로 써 보세요.

I. 1. This is my American friend's daughter.
2. Hi, I'm Min-jae.
3. Hello, my name is Jane. Glad to meet you.
4. Nice to meet you, too.

II. 1. How long will you stay in Seoul?
2. I'll stay here for a week. I'm on the summer vacation.
3. I'll be a guide for you if you want.
4. Thank you. I'd like to take a tour of the city.

Lesson 39 p. 84

★ 다음 글을 읽고 영어로 말하고 영어로 써 보세요.

I. 1. Are there any good places of interest for me to visit?
2. Certainly! Seorak Mountain, Gyeongju, Jeju Island and so on.
3. Can you recommend a good place of interest for a week?
4. Sure! Gyeongju is the best place to visit.

II. 1. Gyeongju is a Korean historical site that is ten centuries old.
2. Really? How long does it take from Seoul to get there?
3. It takes about four hours to get there by express bus.
4. I'd like to visit there.

Lesson 40 p. 86

★ 다음 글을 읽고 영어로 말하고 영어로 써 보세요.

I. 1. Hello! May I speak to Ji-min?
2. This is Ji-min speaking.
3. Hi, Ji-min. How are you?
4. I don't feel very good.

II. 1. Hello! May I speak to Jane?
2. Who's calling, please?
3. This is Min-jae.
4. Just a moment, please.

Lesson 41 p. 88

★ 다음 글을 읽고 영어로 말하고 영어로 써 보세요.

I. 1. Hello! This is Jane. I'd like to speak to Ji-min.
2. She's not at home now.
3. What time is she expected back?
4. In about an hour.

II. 1. Hello. Is this 855-6343?
2. Yes, it is.
3. May I speak to Miss Bang?
4. She has just gone out.

Lesson 42 p. 90

★ 다음 글을 읽고 영어로 말하고 영어로 써 보세요.

I. 1. Hello! May I speak to Mr. Bang?
2. He's talking on another line.
3. O.K. I'll call again.
4. Call again in ten minutes, please.

II. 1. Is this Bansok Foreign Language Institute?
2. No. You have the wrong number.
3. What number did you dial?
4. I dialed 856-6343.

Lesson 43 p. 92

★ 다음 글을 읽고 영어로 말하고 영어로 써 보세요.

I. 1. Hello, may I speak to Min-ji?
2. Who's calling, please?
3. This is Min-ji's friend, Min-jae. How are you?
4. Just a minute. Min-ji, ...telephone.

II. 1. Hello, this is Min-ji speaking.
2. Min-jae speaking. Hi, Min-ji. Are you free tomorrow?
3. Yes, I'm free. What's up?
4. How about meeting at Sillim Subway Station at noon?

Lesson 44 p. 94

★ 다음 글을 읽고 영어로 말하고 영어로 써 보세요.

I. 1. What's the telephone number of Bansok Foreign Language School?
2. Just a moment, please.

3. The number is 2093-3399.
4. Thank you, information.

II. 1. Hello. I'd like to speak to Mr. Kim.
2. I'm sorry. You must have the wrong number. There's no one here by that name.
3. I'm sorry.
4. That's all right.

p. 98

★ 교실 영어 1-영어로 말하고 영어로 써 보세요.

S Good morning, sir.
T Good morning, class. How are you this morning?
S We are just fine. Thank you. And you?
T Fine, thanks. Stop talking, Ji-hoon.
S I'm sorry.
T Did you do your homework?
S Yes, we did.
T Hand in your homework.
S Here it is.
T You are good students.

p. 100

★ 교실 영어 2-영어로 말하고 영어로 써 보세요.

T Hello, everyone.
S Good morning, sir.
T Before class, let me call the roll. Is there anyone absent today?
S Su-hee is absent, sir.
T Do you know why Su-hee is absent today?
S I called her today, and her mother told me she is sick in bed with a cold.
T Oh, Su-hee is coming now. Are you all right?
S No, I'm not. I have a fever.

p. 102

★ 교실 영어 3-영어로 말하고 영어로 써 보세요.

T Good afternoon, class.
S Good afternoon, sir.
T Where are we today?
S We are on Lesson 7, page 18, sir.
T Is there anyone who would like to read this lesson?
S I would, sir.
T Min-jae, speak up, please. I can't hear you.
S Yes, sir.
T Good. Listen and repeat.

p. 104

★ 교실 영어 4-영어로 말하고 영어로 써 보세요.

T Hi, everybody.
S Good morning, ma'am.
T Who is it?
S It's me, Ji-min.
T Come in. Why are you late for this class?
S I'm sorry I'm late. I overslept this morning.
T I'll punish you if you are late again.
S Yes, ma'am.
T Go to your seat and sit down.
S Thank you, ma'am.

p. 106

★ 교실 영어 5-영어로 말하고 영어로 써 보세요.

T Do you have any questions?

S Me, me, me.

T O.K. Hyun-woo, go ahead.

S I can't understand the point of infinitive.

T O.K. I'll explain the point of infinitive once more. Got it?

S Yes, I got it.

T Are there any questions?

S No, there aren't any.

T O.K. Time is up. See you tomorrow.

S Thank you, sir. Good-bye.

p. 108

★ 교실 영어 6-영어로 말하고 영어로 써 보세요.

T We have a short test today.

S Oh, ma'am. That's too often.

T But it's for your benefit.

S We're tired of that.

T Be quiet! Okay, clean your desks. Take out a clean sheet of paper and a pencil only.

T I'll read each question to you. Please listen carefully and write your answers.

T Please raise your right hand if you need to hear the question again. don't forget to write your name on the right hand corner.

T Is everyone ready? Let's begin.

p. 110

★ 교실 영어 7-영어로 말하고 영어로 써 보세요.

T Keep your eyes on your own paper.

S Yes, ma'am.

T If you look on someone else's paper, you will get an automatic zero.

S Yes, ma'am.

T If you don't know the answer, skip it. Then go on to the next.

S Yes, ma'am.

T O.K. It's time to finish.

S Ma'am, wait for a few minutes, please.

T No, you had enough time to write your answers.

S Yes, ma'am.

T Please pass your papers to the front.

S Yes, ma'am. Thank you. Good-bye.